"Ross Farrar's poems are twisted in the best way. Twisted by America, a golden Cadillac, music, and desire. Twisted by Planet Moon and Rotten Sun. That twist is often a stunning torque to the body/mind that wrenches you out of your easy modes of perception and makes something thrilling as a recompense for the cruel and mean. It's like a record that makes you sad, but you must listen to it again and again for its 'terrifying & magical' manner." —Bruce Smith, author of *Spill*, *The Other Lover*, and *Devotions*

"In Farrar's debut collection, the poems' speaker recognizes the world as the place where 'your bad trips are really your good trips.' Moving through physical and emotional landscapes of loss and destruction, 'Ross' begins to understand the inherent beauty in such places and states of being. How do we go on when we lose someone? How do we live between the earthquake's wreckage and the waves invitation to swim? to drown? The metaphorical gun to his own head, 'Ross' chooses beauty, manifested in abundance between the covers of this powerful book."
—Christopher Kennedy, author of *Clues from the Animal Kingdom*

"Ross Farrar is a master of writing about the everyday nothings that ruin a life but also make a life beautiful—the essential mysteries of why you might love someone one minute, and hate them the next, then love them again. And perhaps more importantly, why does death happen to people we love/hate? This beautiful book wraps words around these mysteries so that they give shape to them without straining for answers or false hope. If you are baffled or lost or human, these poems are friendly, slightly drunk companions to accompany you as you muddle through. Read them—there is much comfort in their glorious bewilderment."
—Sarah C. Harwell, author of *Sit Down Traveler*

"Ross Farrar keeps letting us know in his poems: amazing things can happen if we both step up, and he steps up. He shares the freedom of his willingness to surrender to the unexpected. He takes us where we use keener attention to find our bearings. His combination of urgent uncertainty and spoken immediacy, of idiom and invention, bursts with feeling and discovery. Ross Farrar keeps finding what his art requires. To quote Ross's own heartfelt citation of the Gospel according to Wu Tang Clan, Word is bond. In these poems, Word is bond."
—Brooks Haxton, author of *They Lift Their Wings to Cry*

T0124588

Ross Sings Cheree
&
the Animated Dark

•

Ross J. Farrar

Deep Vellum Publishing
Dallas, Texas

Deep Vellum Publishing
3000 Commerce St., Dallas, Texas 75226
deepvellum.org · @deepvellum

Deep Vellum is a 501c3 nonprofit literary arts organization
founded in 2013 with the mission to bring
the world into conversation through literature.

Support for this publication has been provided in part by grants from the National Endowment for the Arts, the Texas Commission on the Arts, the City of Dallas Office of Arts and Culture's ArtsActivate program, and the Moody Fund for the Arts:

ISBNs: 978-1-64605-053-6 (paperback) | 978-1-64605-054-3 (ebook)

LIBRARY OF CONGRESS CATALOGING IN PUBLICATION DATA

Names: Farrar, Ross J., 1984- author.
Title: Ross sings Cheree & the animated dark / Ross J. Farrar.
Other titles: Ross sings Cheree and the animated dark
Description: First edition. | Dallas, Texas : Deep Vellum Publishing, 2021.
Identifiers: LCCN 2020048012 (print) | LCCN 2020048013 (ebook) | ISBN
    9781646050536 (trade paperback) | ISBN 9781646050543 (ebook)
Subjects: LCGFT: Poetry.
Classification: LCC PS3606.A7327 R67 2021 (print) | LCC PS3606.A7327
    (ebook) | DDC 811/.6--dc23
LC record available at https://lccn.loc.gov/2020048012
LC ebook record available at https://lccn.loc.gov/2020048013

Front cover art by Greg Ito | gregito.xyz
Front cover design by Michael Bingham

Interior Layout and Typesetting by KGT

Printed in the United States of America

"Cheree, Cheree. Shut the door, baby."

—Alan Vega

For Michael Burkard

CONTENTS

PART I

PART II

PART III

PART I:

"All my friends in the bad part of town—they're undone."

—Anna Domino

1989

The song went, "Everything the world is doing to me."
Part of you wanted to turn away. How could a world do anything?
Sometimes it feels like the world is sharpening its knife, but
only humans can cut.

The wind turns snow into ice in flight & stings when hits. God,
it hurts. I'd walk home early in March, red welts from weather
that sang *Cheree, Cheree.*

There was hurricane Jerry & Don & Sara & Kyle, etc.
The earth quakes. After Loma Prieta, my father took me out
to the beach.

As we drove, I swear I could hear the crowns of homes cracking—
—people out in the street like 4th of July.

There was smoke, but no fire & the road to Bodega Bay, empty,
nothing broken out on the beach, no fallen, shattered glass.
The human world wrecked behind me & just ahead
waves like an usher pulling us in.

The Rotten Sun

Standing near my grandfather Jack
when he took his last breath, everyone cried
on Dutton Avenue. It was the Rotten Sun
that took him. I asked

my grandmother if I could have his pearl face,
Seiko watch. She freed if from his dead wrist &
dropped it in my palm like new car keys, then I
never wore the thing.

So many years later, Dennis got skin cancer too.
My father called him Layback & he was
our best family friend who always smiled.
Poor Denny shriveled up like a salted slug.

The Planet Moon, unlike the sun, never hurt anyone.
But if deprived of the sun, we become saturnine
& I never went on any of those whaling trips
Dennis planned—

he was overlord of the whales then. Dennis,
you were best when in the sun & I wish you back.
Jack, you were so very handsome.

Youth in Decline

Welcome to the accursed place. The accursed woman
sleeps with the accursed man & they make
the accursed child

& I knew a few of them, may've been one myself.
Willy Pennington where are you? Those dawning years
felt so unclean, hiding under the bleachers or near the train
tracks—no need in sight.

The unredeemable past, it stays there suspended
in time like a tree or a cabin or a bridge
trapped in a plastic snow globe.

The drift is love, yet so hard to catch. I find Cheree
late asleep, high after midnight, well after &
this response: We don't want much else

once we've learned what we're, that we're
ugly & always in a row. But the ugly way
can sometimes be the only way—everlasting.

This is the power of youth. In the streets you scream
& your spirit—you don't know—how it scares
whoever's watching & some go running.
But when I was young, I'd had enough.

Growing

At age twelve, I carried around a copy of the "Desiderata"
in my little velcro wallet & would read aloud when sad.
"Go placidly amid the noise and haste, and remember
what peace there may be in silence."

We have few moments unfettered by sound
& the howls of dogs—what are they trying to say?
There's a blind on the lake that wasn't there before.

A dog's howl sounds like pain, like yearning or
something I could relate. I try to remember the sound.
I miss the people I never met. Look how naturally
things change.

We pray for change & nothing comes. We pray & everything
changes before us like weather. I fell in love & it felt so good.
I fell in love & hated it.

Marin County, Some Year

My mother showed me videos of people helping animals.
The first was a man who raised wounded birds & taught them
to fly, guiding each with his hang glider that resembles so closely
a hawk. Piano music played. It was tender to watch.

The second was a never-before-seen jellyfish in deep water ocean.
We sat on the bed watching it open & close, neon blues &
its pink electric angel hair.

Do you think they have brains? I asked.
Everything has a brain, she repeated.

We watched the jellyfish fly through the water, flapping its wings
on the dark blue screen, breathing in unison, in & out, up & down—
I don't wanna die, I thought.

Future Tropical

We will stand in line under the eaves at Gannon's Isle & see the words,
"Chocolate Everything," but toward the bottom we will see,
"Watermelon Sorbet," which will tear us apart.

A little girl will spray our bare legs with a neon green squirt gun,
her guardian goading her on & a dog will bark at another dog & bite
& bite & the sound will burrow inside us & it will scare
our littlest child & we will not be asleep then.

The people in line will move around each other's desires.
"I want this flavor," you will say, standing behind your budding future,
as the light from Green Lakes sinks deeper still, going bluer, greener—
black.

Waiting at the Boomgate

Why must you step into the canned food aisle
searching the sad cans, too-bright lights all over you?
It hurts to succumb to that.

Wish you were a southpaw like your father. You'd be
more interesting then. Why is your wallet always
in your right pocket & never the left?

Stretch more in the morning, it feels good. Why not do it more?
Put the imaginary gun to your head, a two-fingered barrel,
never one. Why's that? Two fingers more realistic, yes.

These are my years to sleep in the center of the bed,
no Cheree to share it with. Don't you think it's strange
the rich invented money?

You find yourself at the grocery store again, pushing your
broken cart through the sad aisles & in that moment,
you think *you're never at the end*, which saddens you,
the thought.

You hate when people say, "The world would be a better place
without so & so." The world will never be a better place.

& that thing of knowing more about outer space than we do the ocean—
how's it possible to know more about something supposedly never-ending
     & less about what's chartable?

Or the astronauts who traveled around the Planet Moon—
they say how lonely that must've been. Yes,
but it couldn't've been lonelier than this.

Under the Gun of Big Al's

The first job I ran out of high school was at
an adult bookstore at 556 Broadway, in San Francisco,
California. I didn't notice natural life, never stopped
to admire the shapes of trees or the colors of flowers.

I simply waited behind the glass counter & smiled
as the strippers washed in & slipped cheap lingerie
into the mouths of their purses. I didn't look
at the Planet Moon & I'd never.

The way others would stop & point, pumping it up
like some long-dead bicycle tube, since I knew its weak light
would barely reach me, only casting a shadow on my heart

long as ten midnight black Coupe de Villes. How I thought
I had control. Another Martha walking in with a velveteen jumper &
another one thousand people obsessed with our greatest abstraction yet—
love & its backward affections.

Where your bad trips are really your good trips.
How we're never really ourselves at night.

Streets

What had I become?
All that life in me then, a hornet brawn inside my chest
trying to sting its way out & I was making 5K a month,
putting half aside, spending the rest on the same thing.

To ride up Mandela Parkway, right on 11th, left on Wood—
it hid under my green lamp then. No original ideas then
& those junkie roommates of mine were always looking,

so, I'd drive forty minutes north, down Santa Rosa Avenue
to a col de sac fit with rocking houses, parties where
everyone looks directly for you. You're in the bathroom
with the best one. You don't get home. *The police*

will come you have to think & from any vantage point,
raise two fingers, close one eye & aim—bang! bang!—
with the imaginary gun. Don't look at me. Hide the rest

in my sock like it was a novel thing. I'd pass it right over
the bar in a napkin. I'd break it up with a kitchen knife &
smoke a pack of Newports in a half-night, never bothering
with banks, kept it in a metal penguin above the fridge or

in an empty soup box. My sweetheart left me.
I had no love. My friends were all customers & lost
somewhere. I didn't care. I was mean-young.

Mort & Other Payments

I want to pay for everything,
have gotten away with too much. I float through
stations, wade in calming water, fall asleep
with nothing in the way.

A human is an animal with an inside & an outside.
Take away the outside & the inside is left. Take away
the inside & nothing—
mort.

I prepare for death when tying then untying my shoes—mort.
I start out cool on the treadmill & end screaming—mort.
I raise my hand, but can't keep it up there

& I've sat with Beelzebub & those fallen angels
beside the fiery lake & maybe they never fell,
maybe they're rising, getting closer to the big party.

Somehow it feels wrong though. I'm practically cruising through
like an ice cube, colder still the slide's surface & I keep sliding down
the terrible way, too comfortable, no bumps or holes or cautionary tape.

I say no to a bus transfer then find myself
going back into my wallet. I'm responsible. I raise my hand,
tell Ross I love him, but I don't. I raise my hand,
but can't keep it up.

Changing the Light Bulb

I think about speed, the only way to get anywhere in America:
twist. I think about running—right on Broad, right on Lancaster &
down Euclid, until reaching University Ave: twist.

I try to recount the day's events staring up at the bulb, reaching up
to block a light so bright it wills my hand: twist. I try to remember
the faces of strangers I passed, since they're the ones'

I'll meet in sleep. Would I recognize them? There was the boy
with sparkling tennis shoes, a green tortoise on his chest,
swimming. The twins with flattops—ghosts, really.

What's the difference? You see a stranger then they're gone.
How do you know they're real? Their image moves quickly &
the past swallows them like a throat. I follow nearly the entire route

in my mind: twist. I see the turns I took, the mid-section of street
I crossed. Must've been avoiding something? Pausing
in the rose garden, I wonder again what will I have?

A rose bush covered with a cloche that looked like smoke.
Another cat with a bell around its neck, grey feet, must mean revenge——
no, couldn't be.

The Gain of Loss

We say out loud, humans, what should be locked inside us
or hope to be watched over by some great power, say—
the parents of our parents or theirs.

The bad news is that time's running out, it's all about
how patiently you await the inevitable, yet, once you get up,
go forward, that's it—there's no going back.

I overwater the marigolds & they weep. I hold a bouquet of roses
& feel sick. I can't imagine the boredom they feel being looked at &
endlessly adored, each cut & dying flower, their dead, gravid boredom.

The good news is that time's running out.
Life's too long. We have so much time that we choose to discard it
like wet cardboard, changing our hairstyles from long to short,
moving in endless circles & only loving one another in quick,
dashboard instances.

Love might turn us into dogs licking each other's wounds
until they're white & bone-raw. I hate the little chirping birds
in spring & summer mornings,
says Cheree.

Chicago, Some Year

The trains, some above ground here.
When grandma Bette died, I squeezed Anthony
outside a show & cried in his face. I loved
Grandma Bette. The sound of that train
I remember.

The trains, they're just like us.
They get old & need to be replaced
& we need the old to die in order to make room
for the young.

Imagine if nothing died, there'd be no room.
But things must die in order for us to understand
the passage of time.

Burkard asks me if I've ever seen the Rotten Sun
in my dreams & I think *no*. But sometimes
it's always light out in my dreams, as if within
a night of sun.

I took a picture of 200 plus honking geese, all flying
south in a mutilated V, leaving Central New York for the winter
& I felt so warm watching them.

I took a picture of Bette on her seventy-seventh birthday—
her face the color of a peach, glowing
from the candle's bloom. Her warmth
could be felt then as it is now.

Kruk's Silence

When Donald Hall asked Marianne Moore if she missed
the Brooklyn Dodgers after their move to the West Coast,
she replied: "Very much and I'm told they miss us."

& I think they did, should have stayed in NYC—
those poor families of Chavez Ravine. Imagine,
Bobby Thomson fires off *The Shot* in '51

& Ralph Branca watches 3 runs stagger them
like fighters in a ring. But that subway series
wouldn't cease the rivalry. It stayed around,

yet different like how Californians are looking
for gold, while New Yorkers—taxis & I don't think
the Giants missed New York. Their uptown sensibility

remained, although not as blue as Brooklyn & the A's
were still in Philly, so the battle of the bays was just
a figment. In 2010, I'm sitting in class telling myself,

you better leave. It was the seventh inning when
I finally got up, ordered a pizza from Mombo's &
a 6-pack of Red Tails & drove straight to Cheree.

We lived above a karate dojo, where kids were kicking
& punching through the day. We didn't have a TV,
so we listened to Kruk & Kuip' on the car radio.

Brian Wilson throws strike three: "The Giants,
for the first time in fifty-two years, the Giants are
world champions"—Kruk's silence due to tears.

Ross on His Hate of the Man

Birds watch us from above, the tops of our heads like little mops
cleaning nothing. How does such a mag-sound come from such a small
thing? We've deemed it singing, but some birds sound like furniture
being inched across a hardwood floor & always out of key.

But I'm tired of talking about birds. I don't read Whitman. I don't read
Dickinson. I'm more in awe with the patience of laying brick
or how the clock will turn 2:00, 2:00, 2:00 every day until numbers
no longer exist, until the Rotten Sun comes down for us.

I'm sick of nature, all it seems to do is defy me like The Man
& I hate The Man, since I've been hurt by him & his laws
so many times. But then again, sometimes I love to hurt,
how it puts a feeling inside me like nothing else, like feeling

first California rain & I want to start over, to cruise for days
like birds over the sea & know again the thrill of loneliness.

Druggie

Goth is back. Siouxsie & the Banshees are back.
Everything's black. The kids are hot on cemeteries again
& I wonder if every generation was?

They've always seemed pretty & boring, not much there to do
besides stand above death.

I was reading *The Inferno* & thought how nice it'd be
to be remembered as Ross, like Dante—yes.
We're a suffering bunch.

I'd been trying to walk off the 'cid when I found myself
in the gazebo again—no, Archimedes' mausoleum.

Adjacent was a red-tailed hawk perched on a tall grave that read
"FRY" & I was finally starting to come out of that trip.

I suppose this ritual behavior brings us some sense of security, but
from what? Guttering in the dark, above, sky black roof.

Full morning came & the breakfast show was in, stomach
playing hooky, running from the first, foremost meal of the day
& me going back to where I came from, way out in left field
where no one gets laid.

Paul Woods

Paul Woods died today, which makes me wonder
how long I'll sit at his grave & what will I say?
Is there an appropriate amount of time one bends
down? Cut flowers & my friend's body

hemmed in by dirt, etc. I'll stay with you
that long because, honestly, it's all I can take,
"Here Lies Paul Woods. He Tried to Resist"
& I suppose that's the crux.

Who will get your shoes, the vest you wore
for years, burnt orange & so very thin. Would I ever
see someone dressed in you? If I do, I'll approach
& use the code, "Are all cats

really grey in the dark?" You'd tilt your head—
"All cats are cats, Ross. You know this."

1987–2016

When Humans Disappoint

For Richard Speakes

The human walks by. A pack of white-throated sparrows retreat
into the closest shrub. Light carves the day. People do their dishes—
soak the porcelain, soak the glass, let them air dry. The window
is open, say hello, yes—hello.

The human walks by. A rabbit hides in its warren. We take out
our earrings at night, put them back come morning, unplug everything—
plug it all back in, turn it on—off.

You disappear from one thing into another.
I was bagging groceries at Oliver's Market in 2004
then I suddenly found myself in the Swiss Alps
at an alpine chalet near the lake of Sufers.

At a block party a woman approached me & gave her condolences
for my lost cat. I'd never had a cat in my life, but still I said,
"It's okay. I know she'll come back" & turned away
standing over the brie laughing until out of breath.

The Lotto

I started playing the California SuperLotto Plus because I was sure
to win, one-hundred-percent sure, walking into the Quick & Fast
on Center Blvd., smiling & talking to everyone & leaving with six
tickets & thoughts about how my life would go. Still, I wonder

if those tickets brought me in? How much would I give to friends
& family. What if I threw it all away? To Vegas then Mexico &
all the bars on earth. I'd walk into every bar on earth—how I've
lived in bars & I'd be more alone at night than all those parked cars

out on the street or more alone than even the street, more than every
hotel on earth & each of our bodies & all this blood that won't let.
I was sure to win & didn't even get one number—how it called me in.
All those missing numbers & fears of an oxy-sharp demise, of standing

bald-headed & behind the eight-ball. I felt funny, then something about The
Paris Agreement came on & I thought I could stop wasting my life.

Aquarium

Tomorrow I'll be rich.
Tomorrow I'm off, so I stopover in Monterey
to watch the fish.

How their colors disrupt the dull background of the tank.
They're the same old blue & like me
need water to live. They're always swimming.
They never stop.

Like the closet song writer, age eleven,
clock to their back—useless.

Why don't we ever stop? I think.
Unless the net comes down & takes us.
But I fear it'll never come down & my riches,

what if they never come?
& my coffee, what if it's never *really* hot?
The map showing Patagonia, isn't *really* Patagonia.
My closet, full of old pants, not *really* pants.

So, what then? I watch the fish.
They arise from the lava rock & I wonder
if they see themselves in the glass
as I do me.

Leaving Dachau

That cruel reprieve—there stood McDonald's across the street.
I shook deeply. I was there & I'm there again. The victims look like us.
The victims are all of us & nothing there is how it seems.
In front of me always at the wrong end.

The mother inside me wished there to be a daisy chain
around the neck of every kid. "Work will set you free"
& 10,000 dreadful things. So, what are the reasons? Is it our tropism for order,
how someone said, a wallet in your back pocket, change in the front

or are we just potted flowers leaning toward the Rotten Sun.
My mother told me never bring an old broom into a new home,
so when I did it was as if I didn't. The broom, it swept in, leaving everything
old to the new—such a consternation I wouldn't feel until now

& work will never set you free. Since leaving there
no one could speak.

James

To be stricken by people, I confess.
Since we're all born without a choice
& without purpose.

The pursuit of failure as Beckett would feign, where I cry
salt tears over the blandest foods & walk the back-way home,
out toward the island.

There's really only one way to go
as this three o'clock indecision stops me & the afternoon
you take will never be reliable. The younger morning,
how you think it changed.

Why did James ever tell you it'd be his last day?
Since everyone lives in a body surrounded by heat.
You'll wig out at future's end, driving passed houses
of people you love.

Yes, what thrills me is a list too long.
The list will grow. The list grows. James, I love you—
please stay.

New York, Some Year

It was July at the New York State Fair where I witnessed
the most beautiful sunset I'd ever seen. The Rotten Sun
so round & imperial red.

Is there anyone who doesn't agree
sunsets are beautiful? Or is their beauty universal.

Each person looks up & thinks, *Yes,*
I will always treasure you. No, there must be one,

some dark unbeliever, but the truth of any phenomenon
depends on how it's perceived.

I pause at "truth," a word used to describe the absolute. But
over time one truth may replace another.

If the Rotten Sun becomes too hot, the beauty of a sunset
may become obsolete. Sunset Blvd. will be renamed Hell Blvd.
& night will become queen again.

Golden Cadillac at Twenty-first & Broadway

You drive a Cadillac to stick it to The Man,
to state your claim as parade leader, edge into life's continuous
performance, this furnishing forth with big hats & animal coats.

You're guilty of it. But of course, you party on,
laughing at other people when it's really yourself
you're caught inside.

The question then sets: Where is this self I have?
The Cadillac is only itself when people are watching.
When its wheels are spinning, its gold paint catching the eye,

opening wider. It rides with great purpose & must air
a sense of seriousness like that mirrored in its father,
Antoine de la Mothe & his empire Detroit. It all breaks down

after that. There was the motion of love, passing into America,
a swaying, a pogoing, a rapid succession of energy where such sacrifices
Harry Angstrom once spoke, "It takes guts to be yourself" & unfortunately,

"other people pay the price." As the Cadillac grew headstrong,
it always slept alone—glowing in the dark like petals of a young
cherry blossom. Its gait was threatening, its laissez-faire attitude toward

The Man, impressive. We knew this was true when the Cadillac stopped
looking at the Planet Moon. Instead, following it through the night,
into empty parking lots & cul-de-sacs where one can't really escape
themselves, where "The cowslip swallows up the elder" & you idle,
smoke billowing from the exhaust.

Paul Woods Returned

Certain clothes remind me of people I've known or
other shops in other cities. Sometimes, I'm confused
when trying to find what to wear, what to be—
how others will perceive me.

There's the loam Cristian Dior, so soft to the touch.
The dark blue Pendleton Miles gave me, reluctantly,
night of the earthquake. The Calvin Klein button-up
with strange diagonal designs that look like roads &
I think about Porto & its streets I loved—
their dark, cinnamon shade.

The white long sleeve I bought the day Paul died
& haven't worn since. I was trying it on the moment
he went down on his motorcycle, me looking into
the standing-mirror, myself looking back—endlessly.

This is when I sit down. Cheree's in the shower humming
"Heart and Soul." Jimmy's downstairs cutting pages
from a book of nudes. Paul, you're gone & I'm still here
with all of this.

I want to tell you I woke up this morning & felt you here.
But most days I don't think about you anymore. Then
I think about the drive we took across Arizona & into
the Salton Sea, all that talking & when I saw you again
in Nashville, how I wished you'd never leave.

1987–2016

New Orleans, Some Year

We climbed into the Sazerac Bar, into the cognac,
rye whiskey, absinthe, Peychaud's bitters. An orange aroma
filled us like nothing else & no one I loved was asleep.

I started to feel orange, saw it in the wood, in Paul Ninas'
mural that stood against the bars backdrop—in his painted people,
in their skin & hats & pants, etc. We talked about how it's not true,

life doesn't go on for you, it goes off. This is the way we love,
palmy & soon. We sigh a lot, as if what's on the inside
has nowhere to go, laying by the pool again
like animals in heaven.

July 5, 2015

In all my visits to Niagara Falls, I'd not yet stood
on the Canadian side, what some call *the good side*.

An SUV flipped in the main intersection, where I watched
a woman being pulled from the wreck. I could see
her gouged head & blood streaked the asphalt.

The town of Niagara should be mythical & bright
with hanging gardens, halo light, mist.

But sadly, all I saw was gaudy hotels & steak houses,
tourists hunched over railings, crowding around the great hole
where earth eats itself. Sammy had died the day before

& I hadn't received the news until early that morning.
Water spilled in cascades down the ravine, as hundreds
stood beside me on that platform.

It seemed that God had turned on its flashlight, looking for frogs
in the mud, as the fogdog appeared, not yet knowing,
but now I see.

November 8, 2016

I feel young when I hate & often it hurts because there's so much—
hate for me, hate for them. But when I remember to take out the aitch,
I'm simply eating from the past—I ate this & I ate that,
which makes me bloated.

I get a call from Frankie Teardrop & just like that
I'm back in the Panhandle doing bids, climbing through
a window in Chinatown. The Buddha Bar's open.

I hope for a happier year—never change, never change
& drink & we drink. We're drunk again.

A red paper lantern big as four purple hearts hangs above us tonight.
What are all those bleeding hearts doing up there?
The heart is an ugly pump. Goodnight everyone,
I feel very disappointed in us.

PART II:

"I know it helps the times, you asked, though never gave."

—George Andrew McCluskey

Paris, Some Year

I went to visit Edith Piaf at Père Lachaise,
but they had closed the gates early in those days—

& thought about Kierkegaard, how his name means
cemetery, how he lived near one for most of his life,
as if the curse wasn't enough.

A gale of wind through the trees "Give your heart
and soul to me. Give your heart and soul
to me."

First Night of Catholocism

The moment a person leaves, you can feel it, but unfortunately,
they never really leave. They're still out there, somewhere,
carrying on without you, a reminder that nothing ever ends.
Your knees scraped & bruised from the rough floor—
hands open then close.

If I broke it down for you, I swear you wouldn't believe it.
You might fall back a few decades, take your phone from its cradle
& sneak into the bathroom giving five Hail Marys into the receiver
in your chest.

You might make a sign for the cross, pray deeply, ask for forgiveness or
approach the Olympic-sized swimming pool because
sharing the diving board always made sense—
to both dive right in.

But something disappeared—*how?* you think. How do clouds disappear?
They just do, like people, like each of your grandparents & theirs too,
like Houdini's elephant, terribly alone on stage then suddenly—
poof.

This is how it works, you lay there thinking back, waiting for things
to come, when the phone rings & a wave that's been traveling
thousands of miles finally curls over you.

The wave I'm on now is breaking toward some shore,
somewhere. I get off my board, but the tether remains attached
& sand's everywhere, all over me & it hurts to rub—
the rub of time.

I saw you in a cosmic way, milky & long, while everyone's alive today
& those who aren't once were, board in arms, walking again
with no one else.

The Planet Moon & the Potato

The homing pigeon remains faithful to its mate throughout its life &
if they have young, their bond becomes even stronger. Reading this,
I ask myself—*self, why do you find this notion so endearing?*
& know it's because I've always cheated.

Still, I seek the chipped porcelain bowl, the parking space
near the dumpsters, even the pigeon. Some people don't see their beauty—
the gleam of its nape in the Rotten Sun, pavonine like a peacock.

This is how I imagine the potato endears itself to the Planet Moon—
bound to earth, dirty & small, waiting to be pulled up. The potato screams:

If you cut me in half, I'm the same as you, only smaller.
If you cut me in half, I'm the same as you. If you cut
me in half.

Year of the Goat

Passing Magic Mountain tells me I'm approaching
Los Angeles. The bus glides like a manta ray down 5,
where the past disappears & I start again.

I'm en route to revisit Cheree. She's drinking with the filthy
rich—how lopsided the year. I pass a goat digging in the yard

& as I enter the house, we open a bottle of Clicquot & talk about
Bowie & his Spiders from Mars.

We get upset about nothing. Champagne glasses break in the sink &
I think about dying. Soon, I leave the island, wondering if
I'll ever free myself from this human sadness.
Life's a complicated place.

The night becomes a souvenir, how the French say *to remember*
& it sits on a shelf, the night, gathering still

& I know in that moment I've got it all wrong.
How I only live in the future, where nothing's alive yet—
the past, simply a myth.

I pause. Something small & sharp is stuck in my throat.
I cough, breathe—regret.

Cheree at Tenants of the Trees

My human-side wanted to sit against the back wall that night,
near the marae & pray like I do with both hands pressed together
like everybody else.

You might've thought it looked like begging, praying like that. But
then again—what's really the difference?

The people, they were in love with you.
It was your voice, I thought, how it slows down
& blooms at the end of each sentence like our favorite records—
Patti Smith's *Horses*, when the butterfly flaps in Johnny's throat
& he feels himself disintegrate looking out
into the deep.

Rollercoaster

The middle of August in California,
families sitting on the backs of cars waiting for the park gates
to open. It is a hot summer. Cheree tells me
"Death keeps happening like blinking does."
We came for the rollercoaster.

I watch its high point from the parking lot & think about
the feeling of leaving my body—a ghost in human clothes.
It takes hours to get to the front of the line & in that time
I wonder if my fear of electrocution persists.

Clicking up the track, waiting to drop, realizing I've never been ready
for what's ahead. It all comes quickly, without warning, as I try
to free my hands from the bar, watching people ahead
lose themselves.

Thirty-Seven Vibrations

There was a time when people couldn't always see what they looked like.
Light would reflect from the Rotten Sun or Planet Moon—
angled to catch the face looking for itself in water's reflection.

When I broke into Cheree's phone, I knew everything would change,
my eyes scrolling down, words that could've been mine, but they were
someone else's. I must've seen myself there—
the narcissism of existence.

Somehow, we see faces in everything or is it the reverse?
Once, I saw an angel-cloud in St. Helena sweeping
a neighbor cloud across the wine country, a bird's feather
suspended over Highland Park white as a marshmallow.

I kept reading through each text. "I love when you're horny you"
just a rendition of "*I love you* when you're horny." I had to stop at,
"I'll use that on you" just a reminder that we can be anything:
hanging shears in a tool shed or those forever bending machines
I see at the gym.

I shaved my head, cleaned the entire house & thought about saying
thank you for knowing me. But I was no better. I was a savage too.
Downtown, I was faced with the impossible notion of going forward,
unhinged—today then today.

Then I looked at a piano through a shop window. E-minor & E-major
right next to each other, a sad note & a happy note, right there, only
thirty-seven vibrations between them & they started playing—up & down,
up & down—the world round & colorful like a beach ball, floating
& full of dirt.

Daywork

A priest talks to me about God vs.
Pink Floyd's "Great Gig in the Sky," but
it doesn't land. It's their greatest moment, I say.

It's the fear of dying or the cool of dying—
whichever you prefer. People think they're cool
about it thirty, forty years behind,

but what about when it's in the tree house
looking down & you're at the bottom
peering up.

I go for a run because I want to live longer.
But when I run my heart beats a lot. The more beats,
the closer you are to the gig, no?

If you sit inside & don't move, your heart will beat less.
The fewer beats, the farther you are from the gig. The heart,
again, is an ugly pump.

Science would tell us our hearts need to beat hard & frequently
like the wings of a hummingbird. If trees could speak, they'd say
don't move, find a place & grow.

I tell the priest I'd like to die ahead of Cheree, ahead of the ones I love.
I do things with that in mind, like peel the carrots or potatoes,
if I must. I call this *aging* when no one's looking.

Light the candles first. They grow small over time,
their wax bodies trill like sap on a tree & eventually
end up pooling at the bottom, hopelessly peering up.

Costco

Cheree & I wait for the tire to be changed. We call it
a *spare*. We call it a *donut*. We keep calling as the sunlight
comes in through the skylight, mixing with florescent light.

There are no shadows before, in front, or beside us. Here,
we are shadowless. Standing at this desk, waiting for the tire
to be changed, we cannot deny our hunger.

We watch people eat at red, plastic tables & our desire doubles.
We melt under the light the way ice does
in the Rotten Sun.

The Rotten Sun has gotten in & it's melting everything, but
we don't care. We bathe under the wavering light,
waiting for the tire to be changed.

& for once we've nowhere to be. We've come here to be happy,
waiting for things to come, for the tire
to be changed.

Ross in Hell

The minister at Church of One Tree explained heaven
as eerily plain, all soft & grades of blue. In heaven,
I'll smoke again, I think, *but won't have a body to feel it.*

If somehow, I was granted entrance, I wouldn't have
a different life. I'd find a new day each day like I do
now because I can't tell you what's happening
& it feels good that way.

I tell Cheree I don't want to have sex with young women, .
I want her to pretend to be young & we pull this apart.
Desire is our inability to touch the thing.

Why do we love darkness, ending our night
with a serial killer movie? Where ax is delight & sex
is paired with violence. We claim to deny darkness,
yet insist on looking.

Maybe it's all fire up there. They say a body in flames
reaches a state of euphoria before death. Imagine—
all your nerve endings stimulated like that, all your cells
& there again you find a place in the palace of air.

My idea of heaven was waiting around any corner &
jumping out to scare you for all eternity. You always
hated that, but loved it, too.

Year of the Monkey

Arriving at Union Station, I bought you a baby turtle.
James Dean looked sad in his dirty water. The tank too small
& for weeks he wouldn't eat, so you gave him to a friend.

You'd get updates about James, pictures of him tanning
in the pond, getting bigger, "Happier," you said, as the gulch
of resentment widened between us.

That was the year of the monkey, but what do monkeys do besides
swing from the earthly branch, remind us of who we once were?

& those people we were escaped into others, into another's touch,
then meeting after meeting, as if besieged
by fate's constant knocking.

I noticed the streetlights at Union Station, each bulb
enclosed in blocks of fake, plastic ice, decorative
like a star of Bethlehem.

They looked so cold in the Los Angeles sun—
ice that never melts. How we're continually taking in light
from the past, with its yellows & blues traveling homeward
to every room.

Twelve years more & we'd be right back here, monkeys still.
But I wish we could've stayed in those days, waiting for taxis,
replacing holes in the walls.

Pity the Backseat

I didn't wash my hands all day after touching you.
I went through that bus station & into the subway,
then home. There you were, still all over me—
forget me not is how the moment stood.

When I'd lost the feeling, I went looking for it again,
got on my hands & knees & searched in the grass
& in the dirt, so crushed to earth I could almost
touch you.

What happened was simple, I heard the words
rearview mirror & as always went looking
for you in the backseat.

LA Express Carwash

I've been losing so much lately, the designer sunglasses, only had them
a week. I lost the keys to my office, then a library book, *The Dictionary
of American Slang*. A page dog eared at "Garbo: Half an English muffin."
So, I bought ginkgo biloba & tried to stop drinking.

I've almost given up caring about what I have, since it's just going
to be me until I'm no longer. Someone said we only lose things
we don't care about, but I've lost hair & skin cells &
so many prefect days.

We were saying goodbye. You were soon to drop me off for good, but first
we had to visit the car wash. *Mercy,* I thought.

Men in green & white jumpers motioned us in, the wheels catching track,
which made us feel like floating, so we floated through like a submarine.
A machine came down like the leafless organs of climbing plants,
giant soapy tendrils licked the glass.

All I wanted was for the car to stop, for us to sit there in the dark, watching
bubbles on the windshield grow & pop. We bobbed forward,
still trapped, while water evaporated all around us.
Please, let me keep this.

Smoking Parliaments Outside Your Room

At bottom, I knew it wouldn't last, but still
went through & I cherished everything, even your feet,
holding them in my hands like the soft pulp
of papier-mâché.

All those years feeling pink & translucent, as if shinning
a flashlight through your hand as a kid.

There were things we cared about & things we didn't.
How I needed you to call it off. How I could smoke a pack
a day & never regret. How I smoke a pack now
& find it.

Galveston, Some Year

There are instances when a person cultivates the myth
of themselves. In the gazebo again, chain smoking,
you imagine a camera near, as you try to embody
the perfect look, but no one's there.

The lanterns here seem lit with fire that will never go out.
My youth never flushed away from me, constant as these fires.
They flicker in their glass boxes like cage dancers—red hot.

There's a human-sized windmill here, its wheel spins in the warm
island wind. A streetlight casts the mill's shadow, which looks
like a man frantically waving his hands warning oncoming traffic.

I say *man* because this is how Cheree wanted me to act—
act like a man, which meant puffing up my chest to admit guilt.
I saw you looking at them, Cheree said. I know you're not sleeping.
Then the Planet Moon, one day, over-full.

The person I am now waits to stop living like a dog
constantly being walked toward its supposed home
& like a dog, I bury the things I love.

Wag

Ross Farrar, the great rock 'n' roll impersonator,
was out watching thunderstorms in Memphis
when lightning beat out almost cartoonish in shape—
looked like Bowie's face.

Fire moving that way is equally terrifying & magical, for—
it's always better to be hurt than to hurt someone else.

But sometimes you can't help it.
I'm sorry, Cheree.

I heard you call me from across the street
& like a dog went sprinting toward the sound
of my own name.

I don't want a dog for its brains, you said.
I want a dog for its body.

My Dreams Were Never Aimless

In the few instances where I've taken control over a dream, I always try
to fuck or fly. I tell people it's the other way around, but as soon as I see
someone even remotely attractive—well.
Dreams are worthless now.

& I look for Cheree, too, but you're never there. I even tried morphing
strangers
into you, screaming in their faces—*please, turn*!

I saw you in a canoe once, towering headdress made of long, bushy tails &
bull's horn, but they looked older, so I searched for the young version,
brown hair that would've been blonde, but only found bees in the woods—
bananas on a park bench.

Here in life, I sit on this porch & watch buses part the night air
like a curtain & I see you in each one. The busses hum, as you inhabit
the collapsing place in my memory—all strawberry-pink.

I see your face, how I made you hurt & wish I could feel, just for a moment,
how you felt. I see your blue car, but someone else is always driving.

If I ever do see you, I hope I'll know where to go or else pull off to the
shoulder,
getting rid of this Halloween suit.

Listening to the Game

The Giants are losing at home again & I can hear
my father across the country gathering what's left
of himself from the living room floor.

There are worse feelings, I tell him. Viz:
a single curling hair at home on the back of
your tongue.

"Home" is often a word we relate to comfort.
When we're sick we want to be home or after
a long time away we yearn.

I wanna go for a swim, but it's November here & I'm stuck
in the ice. Everyone's gone & time's as useless
as a wet match.

At home we try to sleep in, yet the Rotten Sun rises to console us.
I can wait another day, he tells me & I know I'm getting
older because the easy is getting harder.

Future with Me

At this time yesterday, I was changing the clock. No,
at this time yesterday, I'd be changing the clock in an hour &
at this time yesterday in an hour I was trying to hold onto Cheree
who was three thousand miles away.

Hearing that now is strange because I wasn't actually holding you.
I imagined myself never holding you again & that frightened me.

For a year, I've been waking up in Central New York where squirrels
are black. There are basements in every home & the Rotten Sun
finds me first, me thinking *who are you dreaming of?*

An hour ago, yesterday, I was standing in the past. It was better there.
I was younger, less aware. It's this awareness that really turns me out.
I scratch & pick, look for myself in any reflection as if it was the first time,
so—*what if it is?*

No, it's that I conceive myself as more aware in the future, wiser,
more experienced. But the future is only real in your imagination.
There, you can speed over the limit in cars you don't yet own.
The floors are perfectly swept. You somehow always have the keys.

If my grandparents could stand, they'd tell you there isn't much in
the future besides horizontal black, but I don't agree.

A minute ago yesterday, I was thinking about the future & I can tell you,
Ross, it isn't any better now than it was then.

You still hang up the phone, fitful. You insist on looking, even when
what's in front of you has shifted into its basest form, its darkening bottom.
A year will go, you're never the same.

In the Mud of Apologia

Sometimes it's enough to hear water & with that our Pisces moon.
I wish I could smile. Now, I hear you cry. I turn on the water
& think of where you are. But I'm in Detroit & Los Angeles
is so far away & it's hard to think of anything.

I can barely think. Now I smoke a pack a day. I still
hear you cry. All these tears are mine & you
gave them to me. Yeah, I'm in Detroit

& the Rotten Sun is going down. It's so beautiful here & I think of you.
All these cars go by. I wait for water to warm. I can't forgive myself
for the pain I've caused, so I swim naked in the faces
of those who laugh at me. Time erases the good.

When Aeneas approached Dido in the underworld to apologize,
she said nothing & turned away. You go up all those steps.
You come down. You start on & can't wait for the end.
Everything I was taught means nothing now.

What if you believe in life after? What if you don't?
I wish I could be left alone forever—force the only change
& I remember the smell. I've done everything & everything's
been done to me. I deserve the feeling & every street corner repays me.

It's there, I think of you. When I'm scared
or filled with joy.

Other Streets

Coming in strong from a car speaker, the melodies of Fatima Yamaha's
"What's a Girl to Do?" which sounded sweet. So sweet that Jake
found himself moving to the rhythm. Isn't this what we're here to do?
He said. So very here that I began to sway, too,

dancing in the middle of that swamp-paved street,
hips gyrating & like a plea there came Cheree down the sidewalk,
moving like a crocodile, eyes just above water. But all I felt
was a cold jet & yes, that was it for little ross.

We landed at The Spotted Cat, not yet knowing, but now I see—
"Life is a drag and we are its queens," how Sammy kicked it to me
& the soft pull of Zydeco blues—the disquieted, harkened beat.

Jinx

For a while, I didn't speak with Cheree,
who shared a Pisces moon—what a hoot.
I was them. They was me.

& soon came bent visions, me sitting at a table of lovers,
each person from my past in a somewhat royal position,
elbows planted, knife & fork in hand ready to eat.

I felt like Jesus on Maundy Thursday, a holy bib beneath my chin—
what Kerouac calls: "A frozen moment when everyone sees what's
on the end of every fork."

I wonder now if they saw me heading that table of lovers,
sick with myself, all brimming & robust.

I wished them to see me
for what I really was, a caveman of sorts,
looking for flowers to pluck, place in water with sugar,
waiting the week to droop.

Desire wouldn't let, instead I flared,
big sins fanning out from every pore, for—

I always hurried. I could've stayed, but I waned &
tried to survive—yes. But you know, no one does. Then alone,
I hated being Ross.

PART III:

"The change is cast."

—Lee Mavers

Anthology of Night

One night, tired drunk, I saw a window full of light &
walked toward it. The window belonged to a florist
& on the other side stood a colorful array of flowers.

In front of that window, I felt exposed. I must've glowed
like a wish. I must've glowed from drink.
I must've glowed from the flowering within.

I stood there soaking the flower-view, hoping it would
help me feel better about what's left of me.

I couldn't be sure the flowers were real. Would they
be gone in a week or here for a thousand years?

I imagined they were real, the same way J.M. Barrie imagined
a boy named Peter who could fly & would never grow up.

Then I believed the flowers were unreal. Thus,
reading the dead into existence

We haven't come here to be happy, hope propelling us forward,
pressing our dark-ready bodies into some brief July.

I put my tired face to the glass & stared deeply into the chest
of each flower.

California Jungle Dream States End

On this beach at night, the fat lagoon waves, says
V.O. the night & like the banana moon—*Very Old*—
the night.

Driving over Duncan's Landing, dangerously passed the limit,
the sunroof down, all that energy coming through, every single hair
on my head moved then I felt nothing—
cruising.

Love saying, *without you even less,*
as I felt my will jettisoned—
a thing out in the street.

Moonrise Over Barry Park

Afraid I'm going down the wrong street.
My dreams show me every day I might be
going down the wrong street

or how I should treat those who're real,
who I see in time. Still, I can't help but think
have we arrived?

 I see Barthes' death among the flower pots
& his insistent search for the perfect spice cake.

I believe one should try to be alright, but
defeats stack up & up. Your will leans & tips.

I hear kids playing music from car speakers
& begin to sing.

I wonder what will I have.
I watch the moonrise & must sit.
I blend an undisputable denial with the will to live.

This world holds you up, yes, a place to stand, but
there must be things in this world that only affect in us.

Yet, I feel less attached to what used to hinder me
find myself standing in my backyard looking
into the neighbors, smell their brewing coffee
& start my own.

Around the Reservoir Again

It's the perfect running distance
& with that, picturesque views, places
to stop & drink water.

There are beautiful people on the path, which
reminds me of you. They come to walk their dogs or
to get away from their husbands, wives, partners, etc.
Some stroll with their children. The children see
the shimmering water & blink.

I don't go there to be reminded of you, but I go
knowing it will happen. Fighting, I go most of the way
around seeing you. The times I'd leave happy
in the morning, times when I couldn't love
or thought love was hurt back & forth.

Crossing over Armstrong Avenue & down
that long street, all the houses turning on,
lives people created—what I spurned in youth.

Humiliation.
A person can go their entire life
looking for something in the wrong place,
to the same corner of earth hoping to find
what they might've missed or rather
what they left behind.

Goodbye Forever

A man sat across from me at a public library, legs outstretched
as if at home in his personal space. He was speaking to a woman
on the phone. They talked about nothing, what they hadn't done
that day, "I didn't shower this morning" & "I skipped lunch," etc.

Now, this is something, I suppose, though we tend to call
it nothing because it seems to have zero emotional value.
But lots of things seem to have zero emotional value.

The woman said she needed to feed their child. Thus,
ending their conversation about nothing & in that moment
I became heavy-sad.

Sad in that, I felt no compassion for the hungry child. I wanted
the sweethearts to keep talking & for the child to disappear
into my past perspective where it didn't exist.

I can't apologize for my increasing indifference toward children
I have no direct relation to. I know that sounds bitter-cold,
but it's how I felt in that moment & now I feel nothing.

I'd like children to grow up, so they can know
how much better it was to be young, for them to see me
& my committee of nothing & feel the same bitter-cold for me
as I did them.

Ross on Grief

You associate peculiar things, your mind viciously
trying to attach memory to anything it can, as if grasping
the cliff's edge before falling to certain death.

You open the medicine cabinet & there's the toothpaste they left—
use it & remember. Remembering them, you go to the supermarket
& pass the toothpaste brand they left.

Someone across from you drinks a Diet Coke. You remember how
they used to drink Diet Coke. You see them in your mind drinking it.
Someone drops a word from a sentence like they would.

There they go & you begin to feel as low as the sun in the night.
They've left a trail, so you can find your way back to them, but there's
no way back. That blue car passes. The month they were born.
Almost there.

El Paso, Some Year

We will sit at The Tap drinking before
& after the show.

We will stand outside smoking, women
in miniskirts across the street send
hand signals up to their sweethearts
in county jail.

I wanted to ask them
what they were saying, but
that conversation felt nearly
impossible then.

We will buy something from a man
at the end of the bar then
dance till close.

At our hotel balcony, Juarez laughs
& we cry from it
in our sleep.

Of All the Prisons of All the Oceans

For Dominic Palermo

Eric makes oil paintings of bedlam scenes from movie stills, photographs,
memory. One of a group of teenagers jumping an innocent man.
The blood looks like raspberry jam with its texture of seed.

Another of an American football dogpile, 49ers against the Eagles—
San Francisco urgent & red. A blur of bodies, their gold helmets glossy
& fire-bright. They're always winning.

Maybe all this hurt is just a springboard toward death.
The soul wants out, saying *no* to what it can't comprehend.

I say *no* because *yes* always leads to hurt—a night of simple joy,
of losing myself, alive & nothing else, then suddenly—
poof.
I'm unhappy & I don't know why. Maybe Eric's oil paintings
did this to me—all that hurt & for what?

San Quentin sits on an ocean. I live like that—a prison
on an ocean & it's almost enough to leave, unchained,
all murder around me.

Aftermath

Within the rubble there was nothing left, but the aftermath,
so we kept mowing our lawns & pulling the weeds of aftermath.

The Elysian Fields may be reserved for us in the next life,
or that, yet how will anything grow below the aftermath?

Or on my beach at night, laying out too long under the Planet Moon's
weak light, only to find the skin blue & other hues of aftermath.

This world has been drilled & carved & drained & snapped,
forgiving those who trespassed, near the site of aftermath.

We think we're getting closer to something, bettering ourselves,
forgetting Ichabod's story, his scarecrow-life & that aftermath.

The march continues toward an end, more connected & yet
further alone? & there we sit within two kinds of aftermath.

There was a hunger that grew to such great heights & peaked,
inching & inching toward the back of some throated aftermath.

Ross watched his companion fall away from him, their hearts always
in two & all he could think was *even less* of & the aftermath.

Death Man

What scares me most is what I haven't been in dreams:
electrocuted or married.

I've been shot & stabbed so many times
you'd think I was back in West Oakland,
hiding cash in the tongue of my shoe.

A person can go their entire life looking for something to love, yet
still won't find the thing.

I hold the softening mandarin in my palm, peel back its head
& celebrate its death. I paint my nails green then blue. The color slides.
I open a door to the wrong room.

All of this goes into the lake or ocean or some dark pond
run by snakes & inhuman things.

I haven't been to the beach in so long my body feels deserted,
continually laugh between sufferings, traveling guileless
through time.

Time travel is all about death. You go forward & nothing's alive yet.
You marry one stranger at a time, over & over—
one stranger after another.

You go backwards & everything's dead,
as if it was Yorick holding the head
of Shakespeare.

Let Us Die

Only the young like to think about death. I often
wonder how many times I've passed my death day,
thirty-six times now, but what'll be the exact day?

Will I die the same day I was born like Shakespeare
or just like Uncle Buster, busted from drink, way down
on the floor of his Antioch home.

Will I take the orange Karmann Ghia out, the one
bought years earlier because of a story my mother told me
about her & Candy Finnegan crashing through the streets
of Fairfax in the summer of '69—
still very young.

I'll walk into The Big Four & have a drink then down
the hill to Tadich Grill for another. San Francisco
will be quiet & bare, autumn light creeping down
Hyde Street, through Grace Cathedral which still stands.

Peaceful, but on my way, I'll see everyone, some standing,
some alone & then I'll know I've been nothing.

I'm drunk & there's not many people out. Funny winds
push into the car, but I don't know who they are &
the soft touch of some encroaching thing.

Girl

When you said you lived in Fort Myers, I went back in my mind
to another relationship, with another person, who once lived there too.
I remembered a moment at the Lani Kai, its rooftop bar & swinging
booths that look out over the Gulf.

It's hard to meet someone then to remember another time,
with another person & weigh those experiences against
each other. Memory is cruel like that.

Things ended quickly. That's how my life was then.
I wish I could pray for real, but whenever I've tried
I just ended up deflating like so many days. I would've,
I tell myself I would've.

I think now about that lobster movie where each character wants love
& if they don't get it, they turn into an animal—how ridiculous.
We're already animals, an animal with love, an animal without.

The unredeemable past can only be understood in retrospect—
the way you love something wrong, the wrong way, when you can only
understand what happened after the ice cracks in the lake or when
the telephone stops beating.

Other Pains

I'd come back from the dead of weekends, so high the night before,
the heat from my body could ripen a peach. I thought of Cheree
then dragged asleep

The middle of that night, I woke up afraid, saw something
macabre in the corner trying to break me from my life,
but soon slept the koala's sleep.

Marjorie Perloff says that to perform one's pain is to evaporate it.
If that was actually true, I'd be vaporized by now & surely, I'm not.
I'm here, like the Vitruvian Man, arms & legs splayed out
in all directions, reaching for anything that would have me.

You should've never trusted me. Remember
it was man who created war, without them
there might be peace.

& I hope you never come back, Cheree.
I hope you don't believe me when I say
things have changed, that things are different now,
that things will be.

Waiting to Be Picked Up

Here, in Central New York, rain comes unannounced like a flu.
Outside, the streets teeming with cars, I couldn't get a ride.
Busted, I heard a helicopter & felt homesick.

Envy flew over Athens in Ovid's *Metamorphoses*
searching the earth for any sign of woe, but couldn't find
anything to weep for.

This is when I planned a trip to the volcano. I wanted to feel *awe*.
A word so seldom used in its original: "The power to inspire fear."
Smoke looked like angels pouring out, its lava, lobster-black then
cooked red, which could be love, still—
I wish I could touch it.

It's possible if you loved someone & everyone else disappeared
you wouldn't care. But maybe if you love someone like that
there's something wrong with you. What's wrong with you then,
Ross?

You keep pulling with the claw of a hammer, the momentum
of a last resort, when you should wait for the object to present itself,
as if propelled by psychic jets.

Nothing in the Way

At this point in our history, human history, there's not much
to believe in, so I only believe in sleep.

For a moment, there looks to be a hint of something there:
the supernatural—no, too far out & words, they mean nothing without us.

It's so cold outside that when I die for the first time
I want it to be forever, so I stay in—
"Me at home and you out there,
  along the way."

Waterslide

When I saw the ad for "Mindful Meditation" I cringed,
never wanted any help. I thought I was tough. I saw my life
untethered by other people's devices.

The instructor told me to stay with the breath, that if the mind was to leave
momentarily, it would be okay, natural. This, of course, is what the mind
does—leaves & comes back repeatedly.

There, I saw the house I grew up in, which meant nothing to me then.
How it grew full of water one day, rose like mercury & slid clear from
its foundation.

The only way for us to tell time is by trusting our construction.
There are no time sensors in our brains. Again, things must die & decrease
for us to feel change.

I saw my body, which pushed over time, beginning its little game
of collapse, one piece after another working less, falling away
like paint chips.

I saw a high school crush who's stuck in the year 2002 & started to see all
the other prisoners I've kept, their skin untouched by time, their bodies
trim, each preserved like apricot jam my grandmother
once jarred in the Napa Valley.

California in the past, peppered with fruit trees, that apricot jam would sit
for years before opened—what I'll never know.

I loved the sound of the standing bell, one single tap from the instructor's
hand, where I see people in the room, their resting faces
& the unredeemable past dissolves.

How I Had to Be

Traveling back to my hometown, everything looked the same,
save the trees—they got taller.

Water hadn't fallen that year. The hills a sere, heavy ocher &
some of my friends were dying again.

This was when my smile disappeared & the car really sped up—
predictable, yes?

Like fireworks, we see them coming, the sound we know,
the flower-shape of each burst & without end
they continue to amaze us.

There sailed the blue hair of cigarette smoke inside our vehicle.
Pain ends, begins—goes on like that.

Go slow, I said. A field of cows on my left &
as always, I stuck my head out to moo—
I had to.

San Francisco, Some Year

I cross the Golden Gate Bridge & look out toward
the Farallon Islands, but fog obstructs my view.

I'm drawn to the islands because people aren't
allowed to go there & anywhere people aren't allowed
to go must be good.

This is where they say the great white shark breeds.
Light breaks through the milky-green Pacific, illuminating
them under the ocean's darkening valley.

Where it's as cold as how you said, Ross,
you ruined everything.

Some things can't be removed from the precincts of memory.
I've hoped it wouldn't stick, but it came back like a cough,
words from the hurt-past. Where all I have are a few
bending memories or an island one can only see
on the clearest day.

Catholicism Returned

The night I sought refuge in Catholicism, throwing Hail Mary
after Hail Mary into the arms of any receiver, I soon found
myself in the basement on my hands & knees again. Suppose
Ross was somewhere else entirely, paying too close

attention to *ultimate reality,* as if I had any idea of what
ultimate really meant & this confessional both, always
serving comfort just as much as discomfort, depending on
what side you're on. It seemed an unfair treatment,

like the last strand of floss too short to maneuver around
any tooth & then trying to fall asleep the word would appear
in the night, ugly & bemused: *reality.* God willing, my ultimate
reality was a paradise where I'd never have to truly love myself

& after being with myself for so long I've become tired, faith,
just apathy, given up on everything, whatever could've been.

Walking Through Pages Café

I saw you. No, it was a person who looked like you, same nose & thin,
strawberry blond hair. I could see into your purse, your Frog Prince
Lipstick, an empty pack of Parliaments, one sealed, waiting to be opened.

They had that look you gave I could never parse. Maybe that was it. No,
maybe that is it, when you can't know how someone feels, if they're
beside you or not.

This doubt comes when I begin to question: Why are people so cruel
to one another? How to say I was wrong? If regret could speak,
what would it say? If hope is a thing with feathers—
what's dread?

There should be an empty house or a trough somewhere
I could lap from—a place for loners.

But if I can't go forward, if I can't be free & all I see
is you, sea-change & the vicious past then I suppose
I'm almost there.

Crying

I'd been having a hard time of it, hard in that, I hadn't been able
to function properly. This spiritual cramp, this problem of bemusement
went unseen like dark matter.

So, when I fell asleep that night those feelings must've stayed.
I went back to the year 2013 (at least it felt so), working at the hamburger
place & unfortunately, things felt the same then as they do now, so I wonder—
does this diagnosis hold?

I'd fallen to the ground like people do in the movies & went crying
in a wave. My wails rolled low & as they grew my frequency of pain
grew, too. Until, I met a crescendo, then awake.

What I lost back then (or pined for) was something immeasurable & this,
in fact, has buried me.

The lightbulb above my bed hid in its fixture, unlit, & the insects
sounded like dying things being pushed into my room, surrounding me
until the water welled up inside & wouldn't hold, breaking,
as I broke, too, in the animated dark.

Moving

When comparing tears, my pain is your pain, your pain
is mine, Cheree said. The years are full of empties & the sink,
it shows the same.

The onion has given it to me worse than anyone, Cheree said.
But that can't be true. It was man who created war again—
Sabbath days, working days.

The Divine Comedy starts in the ice of hell, then
into the outer space of ocean, onto the beach, mountains, heaven,
etc. & we somehow look to that for relief. This is our protection
& unfortunately seem to believe in anything that's written.

We look forward to making this place our own
& there are things that take place in the dark between
two people that make everything else go away.

In your mind, everyone you ever loved is hitched.
Then they divorce from the neck.

Lemon Year

After Blue Zero

Something must be greatly wrong. I remember
when chocolate was sexy to pair with wine &
wine with rare cooked meat, how both could be

strangely loved. All the stoners drained their money
on dipped strawberries & those too-hot fireplaces &
nude beaches galore—all of that seems vacant now.

What bruise you hid came quickly back. Think about
the times you had to go in close to understand the thing,
say, the scent of some long-rotten fruit or frenzied ants

atop a dole of sugar. What I've learned in this time:
humanness can be defined by our ability to love, but
the object of human love will one day disappear &

its survivor is the unfortunate one. You step back &
wonder if you're the same person without them & you are—
funny enough. Think about the times you had to

move away to better understand the thing, say,
your faltering relations with distant family members,
how it feels more like an empty swimming pool

or that one-sided friendship that has somehow survived
after all these years & the years that seem to read like
the end, yet, something keeps letting us wake up.

Future Tropic

We will go to Glendale Blvd to watch the parrots sit.
They will move their heads, sensual & slow, or raise a talon
to let us know they are real & we will smile at this.

The window will say "Pampered Birds" & we will think about comfort,
that we are human & want to be touched.

Like the time we danced in Koreatown, how I almost dropped you
during the dip. A naked man played his piano in the corner,
though we were unaware of the water slowly creeping up our legs
& over our heads.

But at that window we will not remember this.
We will only see a false paradise—the violent red of a feather,
the jet-black hook of their beaks.

A woman will open the door to let her children in & again
& again, we will go back to this moment only to find brute change.
The birds repeating a phrase, but we cannot hear it
through the glass.

Acknowledgments

Deep regards and thanks to the following people: Richard Speakes and Karen Walker, thank you for guiding me all these years, for helping me become the poet I am today, and the eternal warmth. My family, thank you for everything, but mostly for staying by my side and loving me when things were unlovable. The Syracuse MFA program, thank you for believing in my work when no other programs did. Thank you to Chris Kennedy, Sarah C. Harwell, Mary Karr, Bruce Smith, Michael Burkard, and Brooks Haxton for your kind critiques. Thank you to my handsome cohort: Bridget O'Berstein, Joshua Burton, Rainie Oet, Ally Young, and James Abele. And most importantly, thank you to Nedda Afsari for standing up against the past, carrying forward and loving me, even though I carry around such a heavy briefcase."

The author would like to express gratitude to the editors of the following publications, in which these poems have appeared previously, sometimes in different form:

"LA Express Carwash," *RHINO Poetry* (2019)

"Future Tropic," *The Chaffey Review* (print, 2019) & *Canary Literary Journal* (web, 2020)

"The Moon & the Potato," *RipRap Journal* (2020)

"The Lotto," "Waiting at the Boomgate," "Moonrise Over Barry Park," "Changing the Light Bulb" *SOVO Magazine* (2020)

"California Jungle Dream States End," read by the poet Brooks Haxton, appears on Ceremony's sixth studio LP, *In the Spirit World Now*.

Ross John Farrar was born in San Francisco and spent much of his young adult life playing music in the band Ceremony. In his late twenties, he decided to go back to school, finishing his undergraduate at University of California, Berkeley, followed by an MFA in Poetry at Syracuse University. His work can be found in *RHINO Poetry, Heartworm Reader, The Chaffey Review, Riprap Journal,* and *Canary*. He has published one book, comprised of literary mixed media, *Society Verse* (Bridge9 Press, 2010), and one chapbook, *The L-Shaped Man Poems* (Matador, 2015). *Ross Sings Cheree & the Animated Dark* is his debut poetry collection.

PARTNERS

pixel ||| texel

EMBREY FAMILY
FOUNDATION

ALLRED
CAPITAL MANAGEMENT
of

RAYMOND JAMES®

ADDITIONAL DONORS, CONT'D

Mark Haber
Mary Cline
Maynard Thomson
Michael Reklis
Mike Soto
Mokhtar Ramadan
Nikki & Dennis Gibson
Patrick Kukucka
Patrick Kutcher
Rev. Elizabeth & Neil Moseley
Richard Meyer

Scott & Katy Nimmons
Sherry Perry
Sydneyann Binion
Stephen Harding
Stephen Williamson
Susan Carp
Susan Ernst
Theater Jones
Tim Perttula
Tony Thomson

SUBSCRIBERS

Michael Binkley
Aviya Kushner
Kenneth McClain
Eugenie Cha
Stephen Fuller
Joseph Rebella
Brian Matthew Kim

Anthony Brown
Michael Lighty
Erin Kubatzky
Shelby Vincent
Margaret Terwey
Ben Fountain

AVAILABLE NOW FROM DEEP VELLUM

MICHÈLE AUDIN · *One Hundred Twenty-One Days*
translated by Christiana Hills · FRANCE

BAE SUAH · *Recitation*
translated by Deborah Smith · SOUTH KOREA

MARIO BELLATIN · *Mrs. Murakami's Garden*
translated by Heather Cleary · MEXICO

EDUARDO BERTI · *The Imagined Land*
translated by Charlotte Coombe · ARGENTINA

CARMEN BOULLOSA · *Texas: The Great Theft · Before · Heavens on Earth*
translated by Samantha Schnee · Peter Bush · Shelby Vincent · MEXICO

LEILA S. CHUDORI · *Home*
translated by John H. McGlynn · INDONESIA

SARAH CLEAVE, ed. · *Banthology: Stories from Banned Nations ·*
IRAN, IRAQ, LIBYA, SOMALIA, SUDAN, SYRIA & YEMEN

ANANDA DEVI · *Eve Out of Her Ruins*
translated by Jeffrey Zuckerman · MAURITIUS

ALISA GANIEVA · *Bride and Groom · The Mountain and the Wall*
translated by Carol Apollonio · RUSSIA

ANNE GARRÉTA · *Sphinx · Not One Day*
translated by Emma Ramadan · FRANCE

JÓN GNARR · *The Indian · The Pirate · The Outlaw*
translated by Lytton Smith · ICELAND

GOETHE · *The Golden Goblet: Selected Poems · Faust, Part One*
translated by Zsuzsanna Ozsváth and Frederick Turner · GERMANY

NOEMI JAFFE · *What are the Blind Men Dreaming?*
translated by Julia Sanches & Ellen Elias-Bursac · BRAZIL

CLAUDIA SALAZAR JIMÉNEZ · *Blood of the Dawn*
translated by Elizabeth Bryer · PERU

JUNG YOUNG MOON · *Seven Samurai Swept Away in a River · Vaseline Buddha*
translated by Yewon Jung · SOUTH KOREA

KIM YIDEUM · *Blood Sisters*
translated by Ji yoon Lee · SOUTH KOREA

JOSEFINE KLOUGART · *Of Darkness*
translated by Martin Aitken · DENMARK

YANICK LAHENS · *Moonbath*
translated by Emily Gogolak · HAITI

FOUAD LAROUI · *The Curious Case of Dassoukine's Trousers*
translated by Emma Ramadan · MOROCCO